Richard Theodore Ely

The Past and the Present of Political Economy

Richard Theodore Ely

The Past and the Present of Political Economy

ISBN/EAN: 9783744645539

Printed in Europe, USA, Canada, Australia, Japan

Cover: Foto ©Suzi / pixelio.de

More available books at **www.hansebooks.com**

JOHNS HOPKINS UNIVERSITY STUDIES

IN

HISTORICAL AND POLITICAL SCIENCE

HERBERT B. ADAMS, Editor

History is past Politics and Politics present History.—*Freeman*

VOLUME II

INSTITUTIONS AND ECONOMICS

PUBLISHED UNDER THE AUSPICES OF THE JOHNS HOPKINS UNIVERSITY

N. MURRAY, PUBLICATION AGENT

BALTIMORE

1884

Copy 2.

TABLE OF CONTENTS.

THE PAST AND THE PRESENT

OF

POLITICAL ECONOMY

"'Ο ἄνθρωπος φύσει πολιτικὸν ζῷον."—*Aristotle.*

"All things whatsoever ye would that men should do to you, do ye even so to them."—*New Testament.*

"Die wirthschaftlichen Zustände und Entwickelungen der Völker dürfen nur als ein mit dem gesammten Lebensorganismus eng verbundenes Glied angesehen werden."—*Knies.*

"Ausgangspunkt, wie Zielpunkt unserer Wissenschaft ist der Mensch."—*Roscher.*

"Durch die Sitte baut der Mensch in die Natur eine zweite Welt, 'die Welt der Cultur' hinein. Und zu dieser Welt der Cultur gehört auch die Volkswirthschaft."—*Schmoller.*

"L'économie politique ne peut rien démontrer sans le secours de la statistique et de l'histoire; car ce n'est qu'en consultant ces deux sciences qu'elle peut apprendre ce qu'elle cherche, c'est-à-dire quelles sont les lois qui ont été utiles ou funestes aux nations."—*Laveleye.*

"When at length a true system of Economics comes to be established, it will be seen that that able but wrong-headed man, David Ricardo, shunted the car of economic science on to a wrong line, a line, however, on which it was further urged towards confusion by his equally able and wrong-headed admirer, John Stuart Mill. . . . It will be a work of labor to pick up the fragments of a shattered science and to start anew, but it is a work from which they must not shrink who wish to see any advance of economic science. . . . Our science has become far too much a stagnant one, in which opinions rather than experience and reason are appealed to.—*Stanley Jevons.*

JOHNS HOPKINS UNIVERSITY STUDIES
IN
HISTORICAL AND POLITICAL SCIENCE

HERBERT B. ADAMS, Editor

History is past Politics and Politics present History — *Freeman*

SECOND SERIES

III

THE PAST AND THE PRESENT

OF

POLITICAL ECONOMY

BY RICHARD T. ELY, Ph. D.

BALTIMORE
N. MURRAY, PUBLICATION AGENT, JOHNS HOPKINS UNIVERSITY
MARCH, 1884

JOHN MURPHY & CO., PRINTERS,
BALTIMORE.

THE PAST AND THE PRESENT

OF

POLITICAL ECONOMY.[1]

I.—INTRODUCTORY.

"THE Wealth of Nations" was published in 1776. Its centennial was celebrated in 1876 with more or less formality in various countries. In England prominent politicians and economists held a symposium to do homage to the memory of its author, Adam Smith. The occasion was remarkable on more than one account. At that time it was the only book to which had ever been awarded the honor of a centenary commemoration; though since then, in 1881, the centennial of Kant's "Critique of Pure Reason" has been celebrated both at Concord and Königsberg. But the chief significance of the event, taken in connection with the discussion thereby evoked, consisted in the fact that, while it brought to light dissatisfaction on the part of political economists themselves with previous economic methods and conclusions, it was at the same time the herald of a new era in political economy. It announced to the world that a revolution in political, social, and economical sciences had already begun, and in various countries had met with no inconsiderable success.

---

[1] In this article will be found extracts from a paper published by the author under the same title in the *Overland Monthly* for September, 1883. The present essay is, however, an essentially different monograph.

5

Nevertheless, in 1876, as at present, there were not lacking ardent defenders of the earlier system. Upon the occasion referred to, a distinguished speaker claimed for Adam Smith "the power of having raised political economy to the dignity of a true science; the merit, the unique merit among all men who ever lived in the world, of having founded a deductive and demonstrative science of human actions and conduct; the merit, in which no man can approach him, that he was able to treat subjects of this kind with which political economists deal, by the deductive method." But the champions of this deductive science had already begun to feel disheartened at the attitude of the public with respect to it; and in the same year, Mr. Bagehot, an equally faithful follower of the old English school of political economy, wrote as follows: "The position of political economy is not altogether satisfactory. It lies rather dead in the public mind. Not only does it not excite the same interest as formerly, but there is not exactly the same confidence in it." And at the Adam Smith banquet itself, Émile de Laveleye, the distinguished Belgian professor, described a younger, rising school of political economists investigating economic problems with another spirit and different methods. Thus were brought together representatives of two schools: the older school proud of the age and respectability of their doctrines, but disheartened at the loss of public confidence; the younger school hopeful because convinced that the future belonged to them.

Although the contest between the opposing parties has continued from 1876 up to the present time, it cannot be claimed that a complete victory has been won by either side. The controversy has, however, been fruitful of good results, inasmuch as the differences between economists have related to the fundamental principles of the science, and new materials have been obtained for that firm foundation which is so manifestly essential to a safe superstructure.

A point has been reached where it is worth while to survey the fields occupied by the opposing forces, to examine the

ground yielded by either party and to ascertain their present
relations to each other; and to do this is the purpose of the
present paper.

Mention has already been made of an older and a newer
school, which indicates a chronological difference of origin.
But it must not be supposed that the lines can be drawn
sharply, for such is not the case. There have always existed
adherents of both parties. Nevertheless, the greatest strength
of the one lies in a time past, that of the other in the present,
and this circumstance justifies the convenient distinction of
the title, "The Past and the Present of Political Economy."

These two main streams of economic thought have received
various designations, each one of which is significant. They
are called deductive and inductive, referring to methods pursued; English and German, referring to the land in which
each had its origin and in which each has attained its highest
development; idealistic and realistic, referring respectively to
a foundation in the mind and to a basis in external nature.[1]
The older political economy is also called classical, on account
of superior age and wide acceptance; while the term Manchester is frequently applied to it, in the designation "Manchester School," reference being had to the locality which for
some time served as a centre of propaganda for its peculiar
doctrines.[2]

Two of these terms, deduction and induction, require further
elucidation, as they have often been used in a loose and

[1] This does not mean that the realistic school neglects the consideration
of psychological motives. It is, in fact, a one-sided designation. It calls
attention to two characteristics of the schools in question, viz., the fact that
the one finds its chief premises ready-made in the mind and has little to do
save to develop them, while the other continually looks to the outside
world for premises. The realistic school, however, studies the mind even
more carefully than the idealistic, and corrects its imperfect psychology.
The realistic is also idealistic, in the sense that it attempts to realize high
ideals.

[2] Other more special designations of the newer school are mentioned
further on, where its principles are discussed.

unintelligent way, and especially as the leaders of the two
directions seem to be in doubt concerning their real purport,
the same writer being called now deductive, now inductive,
while other investigators appear at a loss to know which to
style themselves. The extent of this confusion is made evident by the perusal of works like Cairnes's " Character and
Logical Method of Political Economy " and Jevons's " Theory
of Political Economy." As Professor Jevons points out,
induction does not preclude deduction, and an entire absence
of deduction is to be found in no treatise on political economy
and in no economic monograph. However, deductive is
applied to that political economy which, taking its ultimate
facts, its premises, from other sciences, from common and
familiar experience, or from the declarations of consciousness,
proceeds from these and from definitions to evolve an economic
system without any further recourse to the external world,
save perhaps as furnishing tests of the validity of the reasoning. That was the character of the classical English political
economy of which a good illustration is furnished by Nassau
Senior's treatise on " Political Economy." [1] " The premises of
the political economist," says this writer, " consist of a very
few general propositions, the result of observation or consciousness, and scarcely requiring proof, or even formal statement, which almost every man, as soon as he hears them,
admits as familiar to his thoughts, or at least as included in
his previous knowledge; and his inferences are nearly as general, and, if he has reasoned correctly, as certain as his premises." Elsewhere Senior speaks of the "undue importance
which many economists have ascribed to the collection of
facts."

The term inductive, on the contrary, is to be applied to
those writers who do not start out with *all* their premises ready
made, but who include the induction of premises within the
scope of their science and proceed to use these premises deduc-

[1] 6th Ed., London, 1872.

tively. The inductive political economist, for example, gathers together particular facts relating to the effects of the division of labor upon production, or facts respecting government and private banks; and observing particulars in which these facts agree among themselves, separates out these similars and forms what we call a generalization. This serves him in future for a major premise in economic reasoning. The inductive political economist compares his conclusions with external facts, not simply for the sake of testing the accuracy of his reasoning, but also in order to ascertain whether the generalization itself was made on sufficient grounds. It is difficult to ascribe any other meaning to induction which is not obviously absurd. Nothing, indeed, could be more ridiculous than to gather economic facts at hap-hazard and to catalogue them as gathered. If induction means that, then what Cairnes writes of the inductive economist would be indisputable: "He may reason till the crack of doom without arriving at any conclusion of the slightest value."[1] But no one ever supposed induction to mean such sheer nonsense. The inductive economist starts with some hypothesis to serve as a guiding thread in the bewildering labyrinth of facts. He generalizes in order to observe, but likewise observes in order to generalize.

II.—The Old School.

Leaving out of consideration Adam Smith, to whose inspirations all economists trace their origin, the leading representatives of English political economy are Malthus, Ricardo, Senior, and the two Mills, James and his son John Stuart. These writers contributed various parts of that economic system, which the epigones in political economy contemplate with awe and admiration as something not to be questioned, and which reigned almost supreme in England and in literary and

---

[1] "Character and Logical Method of Political Economy."—2nd. ed., London 1875, p. 65.

learned circles in all Christendom until within twenty or
thirty years. It acquired the reputation of orthodoxy, and to
be a heretic in political economy became worse than to be an
apostate in religion; and even to-day in France this entirely
unscientific conception of orthodoxy plays such a rôle that it
is considered complimentary to apply the predicate orthodox
to a distinguished economist.

These men generally opened their text-books with a definition of political economy. Their definitions differed in a few
minor respects, but finally attained a form which was commonly accepted; and it may be well to preface the more
detailed account of their system with this definition. It reads
as follows: " Political economy is the science which treats
of the production, distribution and exchange of wealth."
This definition furnishes the most general view of their
political economy.

The teachings of this school were comparatively simple,
especially as found in the systematized expositions of their
adherents, who followed after them, and at a very long distance
behind them. Their doctrines were chiefly and considered as
a whole, deductive and flowed naturally from a few hypotheses concerning human nature and the external physical world;
and these hypotheses served as the ultimate premises of economic science. That universal self-interest, or, as the epigones
coarsely and with exaggeration styled it, universal selfishness,[1]
was the animating and overwhelmingly preponderating cause
of economic phenomena, constituted the leading assumption
of this English or Manchester school of political economy.
"The Wealth of Nations," says Buckle, one of the Manchester men, "is entirely deductive, since in it Smith generalizes the laws of wealth, not from the phenomena of wealth,
nor from statistical statements; from the phenomena of selfishness." While it is possible to maintain, with considerable show

---

[1] That it was a decided error to identify self-interest and selfishness is
pointed out further on in this monograph.

of plausibility, that this is far from being a correct interpretation of Adam Smith, it most undoubtedly represents teachings of followers, who pushed their tendencies in method and doctrine to an extreme. Smith, indeed, made use of history and statistics, but this was not done by Ricardo, his most distinguished disciple, and the corypheus of English classical political economy. The latter opens his work on "Political Economy and Taxation" with a discussion of "Value." In all that he says concerning it—and that means twenty-five large octavo pages—he does not adduce one single illustration from actual life. Not even one historical or statistical fact is brought forward to support his conclusions. No mention is made of a single event which ever occurred. It is really astounding when one thinks of it. The whole discourse is hypothetical. "Suppose now a machine," writes Ricardo in one place, "which could, in any particular trade, be employed to do the work of one hundred men for a year, and that it would last only for one year. Suppose, too, the machine to cost £5,000, and the wages annually paid to one hundred men to be £5,000, it is evident that it would be a matter of indifference to the manufacturer whether he bought the machine or employed the men. But suppose labor to rise and consequently the wages of one hundred men for a year to amount to £5,500, it is obvious the manufacturer would now no longer hesitate; it would be his interest to buy the machine, and get his work done for £5,000. But will not the machine rise in price? . . . . It would rise in price, if there were no stock employed in its construction. . . . . If, for example,"—and, in this strain, which sufficiently illustrates his style and method, Ricardo continues indefinitely. Inside of two pages, he introduces no fewer than thirteen distinct suppositions, all of them purely imaginary.

A second leading hypothesis of this older school has been variously expressed. In its most objectionable form it asserted that a love of ease and aversion to exertion, was a universal characteristic of mankind.[1] In its least objectionable form it affirmed the universality of the desire to attain a maximum of effect with a minimum of sacrifice; or, as it is still better expressed by Cairnes, "the intellectual power of judging of the efficacy of means to an end, along with the inclination to reach our ends by the easiest and shortest means." These two statements differ considerably; in fact to such an extent that it is doubtful whether they ought to be regarded as expressions of essentially similar proportions. As first stated the principle would antagonize the desire for wealth, one of the manifestations of selfishness; in the second form it simply means that no needless exertion will be expended in attaining an end. More wealth is balanced against additional sacrifice of ease and wealth.

A further hypothesis was the absolute lack of friction in economic movements. Not only do capital and labor move with perfect ease from place to place and from employment to employment, but this, it was implicitly maintained, is accomplished without the slightest loss. The silk manufacturer diverts his capital into another employment like the construction of locomotives with precisely the same facility with which he turns his family carriage horse from an avenue into a cross street, while the Manchester laborer on a moment's warning finds a suitable purchaser for his immovable effects and without expense or loss of time transfers himself to London where employment is at once offered him at the rate of wages there current. Equality of profits and equality of wages flowed naturally from these assumptions.

An additional common premise of the older political economy was this proposition: The beneficent powers of nature or the "free play of natural forces" arrange things so that the

---

[1] In his article entitled "Recent Attacks on Political Economy," (*Contemporary Review*, Nov., 1878), Mr. Lowe (Lord Sherbrooke) declares that "wealth and ease" are the only two premises of political economy and says that the whole science is based on "the absolute supremacy of the desire of wealth and aversion from labor" (p. 864).

best good of all is attained by the unrestrained action of self-interest. This was taken from Adam Smith, who often gave expression to this view.¹ A hundred quotations similar to this might be adduced: "Every individual is continually exerting himself to find out the most advantageous employment for whatever capital he can command. It is his own advantage, indeed, and not that of the society which he has in view. But the study of his own advantage *naturally* or rather *necessarily* leads him to prefer that employment which is most advantageous to the society."

The perfectly logical conclusion drawn from this hypothesis, was that government should abstain from all interference in industrial life. *Laissez-faire, laissez-passer*—let things alone, let them take care of themselves,—was the oft-repeated maxim of *à priori* economists.

This was a part of a general conception of the naturalness of things as they existed in modern industrial society, a conception which may be traced back through French eighteenth century philosophy to the theory of Roman jurisprudence, and which is thus described by an unquestioning adherent.² This industrial world "is governed by natural laws, admirable laws, in many respects inflexible, which it is necessary to know and respect. . . . . These laws are superior to man. Respect this providential order; let alone the work of God. . . . . This maxim, *laissez-faire, laissez-passer*, is one of the most beautiful, one of the most profoundly philosophical and at the same time one of the most just which have been brought forward in a long time. It carries with it the revelation of

---

¹ In other parts of his work, Adam Smith gives expression to views, whose tendencies are quite different. The general bearing of the Wealth of Nations is, undoubtedly, optimistic, though pessimists can find support in places. The "School of Harmony" was a later product, due more to Henry C. Carey than to anybody else. It is now generally recognized that a great deal of what Bastiat put forth as original was taken from Carey.

² Ch. Coquelin, in his article on Économie Politique, published in the Dictionnaire d'Économie Politique.

our science and announces the presence of those natural laws,
which it is the mission of the science to study. At the same
time this maxim is the first fruit of this revelation."

Thus it is that the dignity of natural law is conferred upon
all these hypotheses by the classic political economy of the
past. They hold good, it is upheld, for all places and for all
periods of time, and the same universal character must attach
to the deductions from them, consequently, to the entire
science of political economy.

Has not man, it was further argued in proof of this, ever been
actuated by self-interest? Has he not ever been obliged to labor
in order to satisfy the wants of his nature? Was there ever
a time he did not need food and shelter? Does not the
very instinct of childhood set apart certain things like toy-
horses, wagons, and even a corner of a room or of a sofa, and
attribute to them a peculiar quality in pronouncing them
"mine"? And can we go back to a period of time when
this unchangeable human nature of ours in its immutable
desire of ownership of the essentials of well-being did not
lead to the institution we call private property? Is not the
multiplication of the human species a universal law? Is
Nature in this respect one whit different in France from what
she is in Germany or England, or in Ethiopia from what she
is in the United States? Or is it possible to discover a
divergence between her processes among the Egyptians four
thousand years ago and those which to-day obtain in Spain
or Portugal? Is not this competition, which we see going
on about us every day, an eternal law of Nature? Is it not a
necessary and inevitable consequence of the fundamental fact
of limitation of objects suitable to the satisfaction of our
desires and the universal principle of self-interest, which
prompts each individual to satisfy, in the most complete manner, his own desires,— in other words, to obtain more than his
proportional share of the limited store of goods? Is not
wealth itself an object "distinct, necessary, permanent and
universal," such an object as fits it to be the subject of scien-

tific investigation? Are not these words of Courcelle Seneuil a correct description of wealth? "We can discover neither group of men nor individual able to live without making use of a greater or less amount of wealth, without possessing a power more or less extended over the exterior world. This is true in all times and in all latitudes. In whatsoever condition we consider man we find him besieged with wants which he must satisfy under pain of death and which he can only satisfy by means of objects whose possession constitutes his wealth."

Political economy can then have no connection with government. It treats of the universal desire of wealth, an object "distinct, necessary, permanent, and universal," the natural causes and processes of its production and distribution. It can likewise then have as little connection with nationality as physics, and "there is no more a French, or German, or American political economy or political science than there is a French, or German, or American science of astronomy or chemistry."[1]

To put it positively, the political economy of the past was a pure science, which was considered apart from policy, which as a changeable, fluctuating factor, introduced a disturbing element into what was otherwise immutable. "Until economical questions," writes an adherent of this method in *The Nation*, "are considered and answered from a purely scientific standpoint without respect to any considerations of policy, it is vain to hope for any decided advance in our means of judging them." That is to say, political economy is a science in an older and narrower sense which limits science to the discovery of truth without regard to its practical applications.[2]

---

[1] Preface to the Cyclopædia of Political Science, Political Economy and United States History.

[2] An interpretation of science, formerly much commoner than to-day, is that given by Mr. Robert Lowe in his article on the Recent Attacks on Political Economy, in the *Nineteenth Century* for November, 1878. He finds the crucial test of science in the power of prediction. The

Indeed one writer, M. Coquelin,[1] has gone so far as to say that political economy as a science—and as such he maintains it should be cultivated—has no purpose. "Science does not counsel, order, or prescribe; it confines itself to observation and explanation."

It must not be supposed that this entire statement of economic premises would find acceptance with any one writer of the older school, nor that there are no differences of opinion among those thus classed together. This is far from the true state of the case. There are numerous subdivisions, or sects, in this older school, and sometimes these minor divisions are called schools, though less properly; for a school of thought refers to the foundation-principles of a science. Nevertheless wide differences are found among the older economists. Some, like Bastiat, accept the doctrine of harmony of interests, to which reference has been made, and carry it to its logical outcome, while others, like Ricardo, develop strong pessimistic tendencies. But what has been said characterizes the drift of one main stream of economic thought.

Nassau Senior has summed up, under four heads, the premises of political economy, as he understands them, and it may be well to quote his statement in this place.

The propositions alluded to are these:

" I. That every man desires to obtain additional wealth with as little sacrifice as possible.

"II. That the population of the world, or, in other words, the number of persons inhabiting it, is limited only by moral or physical evil, or by a fear of a deficiency of those articles of wealth which the habits of the individuals of each class of its inhabitants lead them to require.

"III. That the powers of labor, and of the other instruments which produce wealth, may be indefinitely increased

---

writer denies that science means more than systematized knowledge. The power of prediction which any branch of knowledge may convey with it, can be known only when the science is completed.

[1] *Vide* Art., Économie Politique in the Dictionnaire d'Économie Politique.

by using their products as the means of further production."

This third proposition simply asserts the productivity of what is ordinarily called capital.

"IV. That agricultural skill remaining the same, additional labor employed on the land within a given district produces, in general, a less proportionate return, or, in other words, that, though with every increase of the labor bestowed, the aggregate return is increased, the increase of the return is not in proportion to the increase of the labor."

This fourth proposition is commonly known as the law of diminishing returns, and as such is familiar to every political economist.

III.—The Attractions of Economic Orthodoxy.

The attractions of these doctrines were numerous and evident. For the confusing, the bewildering complexity of the economic phenomena surrounding us, they substituted an enticing unity and an alluring simplicity. They appealed irresistibly to the vanity of the average man, as they provided him with a few easily managed formulas, which enabled him to solve all social problems at a moment's notice, and at any time to point out the only true and correct policy for all governments, whether in the present or the past, whether in Europe or Asia, Africa or America. It required, indeed, but a few hours' study to make of the village schoolmaster both a statesman and a political economist. Neither high attainments nor previous study and investigation were required even in a professor of the science. "Although desirable that the instructor should be familiar with the subject himself," writes Mr. Amasa Walker in the preface to his "Science of Wealth," "it is by no means indispensable. With a well-arranged text-book in the hands of both teacher and pupil, with suitable effort on the part of the former and attention on the part of the latter, the study may be profitably pursued.

2

We have known many instances where this has been done in colleges and other institutions, highly to the satisfaction and advantage of all parties concerned."

Ordinarily the search for new truth is considered a fascination. As the old proverb has it, it is the chase and not the game which attracts the hunter; and scientists generally find their specialties interesting, in proportion as there remains truth to be discovered and in proportion to their estimate of the probability that they will be successful in the pursuit of this undiscovered truth. But political economists of the past have aspired to add a new attraction to their study in pronouncing it perfect and complete, or at any rate very nearly so. Their pride in the possession of final truth has stifled their curiosity; and clothed upon with the armor of infallibility they have constituted themselves popes in the domain of science and hurled their anathemas at dissenters.

Now that everything in political economy seems unsettled it is curious to read the expressions of those who, twenty, thirty and forty years ago, thought this branch of knowledge full grown and devoid of blemish.

Nearly sixty years ago M'Culloch wrote these words in his "Principles of Political Economy:" "Political Economy has not been exempted from the common fate of the other sciences. None of them has been instantaneously carried to perfection; more or less of error has always insinuated itself into the speculations of their earliest cultivators. But the errors with which political economy was formerly infected have now nearly disappeared; and a very few observations will suffice to show that it really admits of as much certainty in its conclusions as any science founded on fact and experiment can by any possibility do."[1]

In a still earlier work by Colonel Torrens, the following words are to be found: "In the progress of the human mind, a period of controversy amongst the cultivators of any branch

---

[1] Political Economy, Part I.

of science must necessarily precede the period of unanimity. With respect to political economy, the period of controversy is passing away, and that of unanimity rapidly approaching. Twenty years hence there will scarcely exist a doubt respecting any of its fundamental principles."[1]

And more than twenty years later, even John Stuart Mill wrote as follows respecting the laws of value:[2] "Happily there is nothing in the laws of value which remains for the present or any future writer to clear up; the theory of the subject is complete; the only difficulty to be overcome is that of so stating it as to solve by anticipation the chief perplexities which occur in applying it."

Alas for the vanity of human prophecy! The controversial matter which has been written on value since John Stuart Mill penned those words would, it is safe to affirm, fill many a large octavo volume. And even now economic views respecting value are far from harmonious.

Another attractive feature of this economic system was the favor it gained for its adherents with existing powers in state and society. No exertion, no sacrifice, was required on their part to alleviate the sufferings of the lower classes. They were simply to let them alone and go their way, convinced that they were most truly benefiting others in pursuing their own egotistic designs. The capital of the country was divided according to fixed and unalterable laws into two parts: the one designed for laborers, and called the wage-fund; the other destined for the capitalists, and called profits. So far, nothing was to be done, because nothing could be done. It was impossible to contend against nature. If you should thrust her out with a pitchfork, she would return. Moreover, competition distributed the two portions of capital justly among the members of the classes for whom they were

---

[1] Quoted by Cairnes from Torrens's "Essay on the Production of Wealth." 1821.

[2] Political Economy, Book III, Chapter I.

designed: the wage-fund equally and equitably among the
laborers, the profits equally and equitably among the capitalists.   Even Cairnes thinks the decrees "ordinarily given
to the world in the name of political economy," amount in
the main "to a handsome ratification of the existing form of
society as approximately perfect."[1] Such bright, rose-colored
views so influenced some that they began to talk about the
"so-called poor man," and at times appeared to think an
economic millennium about to dawn upon us. It was only
necessary to pull down a few more barriers and allow still
freer play to natural forces.

IV.—MERITS OF THE OLD SCHOOL.

Whatever views we may entertain of the correctness of the
doctrines described, we should not fail to recognize the
merits of the orthodox English school of political economy—
the classical political economy. It separated the phenomena
of wealth from other social phenomena for special and separate study. It called attention to their importance in national
life. It convinced people that it was folly to attempt to
understand society without examining and investigating the
conditions, the processes, and the consequences of the production and distribution of economic goods. Even if it was an
error to attempt to study these economic phenomena by themselves, entirely apart from law and other social institutions, the
effort was of importance as bringing out this very impossibility.
If it was an error to assume simplicity of economic phenomena,
the error itself led to an investigation of them, from which
people might have been deterred, if their complexity and
difficulty had been sufficiently realized.

Again, the construction of a deductive science of human
actions even upon insufficient premises was a labor of high
merit and required minds of the first order. The intelligent

---

[1] Character and Logical Method of Political Economy, p. 25.

perusal of Ricardo's Political Economy is more difficult to
the average college student than the mastery of his Euclid.
Premise follows premise and conclusion conclusion in an
unbroken logical chain, extending through the entire work;
and the loss of any link in the argument at once renders the
text incomprehensible. The study of this author's writings
is undoubtedly excellent mental discipline.

Further, the present political economy in all parts of the
world grew out of the classical political economy, and the
former cannot be comprehended until the latter has been
mastered. It was indeed efforts to master, extend and perfect
the older school, as well as other causes like later develop-
ments of industrial life, which gradually led to the most
recent economic investigations. Nor does any one now doubt
the continued and all-pervading—even if not all-controlling—
influence of those motive powers, which furnished Ricardo,
Mill and Senior with their major premises; but this fact was
not understood before the coryphei of the older political
economy elucidated it, and they deserve great credit for what
may be fairly termed their discoveries. It was, for example,
a service of no mean order, to point out all the ramifications of
self-interest in economic life, to set in order the phenomena
explained by this principle, and to show how it prompts men
to the most diverse deeds, which, undertaken without a view
to the welfare of others, nevertheless redound to the common
good. And it must be confessed that no single principles
have been discovered by the German school, which throw such
a flood of light on the multifarious phenomena of economic
life as do, for example, the Ricardian theory of rent, and the
Malthusian doctrine of population.

The services rendered by economists of this school in practical life were not less important. They were instrumental in
tearing down institutions, which, having outlived their day
and usefulness, were simply obstructions to the development
of national economic life. This happened in many lands, but
it is necessary to enumerate only a few examples. The Baron

vom Stein was the man of all others who ushered in the era
of modern political institutions in Prussia.   He began his
career as minister by demolition.   As Seeley, in his "Life and
Times of Stein," admits with more good sense than usually
characterizes English writers on free trade and protection,
international free trade was not to be contemplated in the
countries of continental Europe.   It was only to be thought
of in countries like England—"shielded comparatively from
war, and depending upon foreign countries for its wealth."
But internal free trade, *i. e.*, free trade within the nation
itself, was both practicable and advisable.   Stein accordingly
abolished, early in the century, the internal customs, which
had proved a great hindrance to trade and industry, while
yielding the state the insignificant sum of some $140,000 per
annum (Part I. Chap. V. p. 100 [1]).   Restrictions on the transfer
of land and serfdom were institutions which stood in the way of
a desirable national development, and both were abolished by
Stein's celebrated Emancipation Edict of 1807 (Part III.
Chap. IV.).   While he was influenced considerably by Tur-
got's writings and practical activity as governor of a province
and Minister of Finance, he expressly acknowledges that he
studied Adam Smith's "Wealth of Nations," and was guided
by it in his policy (Part I. Chap. V. p. 99).   I have mentioned
only three cases where English political economy influenced
German national life.   These would be important enough to
attract attention if they were the only instances, whereas its
influence has not ceased at the present time.   There still
exists in Germany a society of men called the Economic Congress, founded in 1858.   They represent the extreme
economic views of the old school, and endeavor to bring legislation into harmony with their ideas; and their efforts in the
past have been by no means altogether fruitless.

    It is less necessary to describe the practical effects of the
orthodox political economy in England.   It began by influ-

---

[1] Seeley's Life and Times of Stein.' Boston.   1879.

encing the younger Pitt, and reached its culmination, perhaps, in the introduction of international free trade under Cobden and Bright.   It has now been explained what the older English political economy was, and what it accomplished both for science and practical life.   It is next necessary to show how it broke down both as a scientific system and as a political guide, and to describe the origin, growth, and character of the modern school of political economy.

V.—The Decline and Fall of the Old School.

It must be noticed first that the whole spirit of its practical activity was negative.   It was powerful to tear down, but it did not even make an attempt to build up.   Like the anarchists, it assumed the existence in nature apart from man's will, of a sufficient constructive power.   In many respects it resembled the French revolution, and it was hailed with joy for the same reason.   They both represented the negative side of a great reform, and as such answered the needs of the latter part of the eighteenth and the earlier part of the nineteenth centuries.   The ground had to be cleared away to make room for new formations; and the system of political economy described could not endure permanently because in its practical workings it was *only* negative.   It had nothing to say when industrial progress and new economic formations brought to the front fresh problems for solution.   It was obliged to give way to a school which should attempt the positive work of reconstruction.   It failed first as a guide in industrial life, and it is this failure which must now occupy our attention.

Let us consider at the outset that phrase, which contains the quintessence of its advice to the statesman and which has been lauded as the revelation of our science as well as of the providential and inflexible order of the industrial world. The phrase referred to is, of course, *laissez-faire, laissez-passer.* It never held at any time in any country, and no maxim ever made a more complete fiasco when the attempt was seriously made to apply it in the state. The truth is, the stern necessities of political life compelled statesmen to violate it in England itself, even when proclaiming it with their lips. This was first done apologetically, and each interference was regarded by the "school" as an exception to the rule; but it finally began to look as if it were all exception and no rule. Interference was found necessary in every time of distress, as during our late civil war, when government borrowed money for public works to give employment to the Lancashire operatives, at the time of the cotton famine. Every reform in the social and economic institutions of Great Britain has been accomplished only by the direct, active interference of government in economic affairs. When Gladstone began his work of conciliating Ireland in 1869, he found it expedient to grant loans of public money to occupiers who wished to improve their holdings, and to proprietors to reclaim waste lands or to make roads and erect buildings, enabling them thereby to employ labor. In 1880 the government of Ireland again decided to alleviate the sufferings of the Irish, by making an advance of £250,000 out of the surplus of the church funds, for public works of various kinds, in order to provide employment for those needing it. The recent Irish acts interfering between tenant and landlord in the matter of rent, and offering the assistance of the state to tenants in arrears, violate all the principles of *laissez-faire* economists, and are nevertheless applauded by the wisest and best men of all lands. *Laissez-faire* was tried in the early part of this century in English factories, with results ruinous to the morality of women and destructive of the health of children. Robert Owen, himself a large and successful manufacturer, declared that he had seen American slavery, and though he considered it bad and unwise, he regarded the white slavery in the manufactories of England as far worse. Children were then—that is, about 1820—employed in cotton, wool, silk, and flax establishments at six and even five years of age. The time of labor was not limited by law, and was generally fourteen, sometimes fifteen, and in the case of the most avaricious employers even six-teen hours a day; and this in mills sometimes heated to such a degree as to be injurious to health. I know of no sadder reading and no more heart-rending tales than appear in the government reports on the condition of the laboring classes previous to state interference in their behalf in England. The moral and physical degradation of large classes was shown, by undisputed testimony, to be such as to put to shame any country calling itself civilized and Christian. · It could scarcely be surpassed, even if paralleled, by the records of savage and heathen nations.

Government began to interfere actively in behalf of the laborers in 1833, and since 1848 has largely extended its protection. The time of labor has been limited, and the employment of women and children regulated by a Factory Act, which is regarded as a triumph of civilization; if the "*London Times*," and Mackenzie's work, "*The Nineteenth Century*," can be trusted, investigations show that the act has proved an "unmingled good." And Stanley Jevons uses this still stronger language: "This Consolidation Act is one of the brightest achievements of legislation in this or any other country." [1] Sanitary legislation has improved the dwellings, health, and morality of the poorer city population. Govern-ment spent, *e. g.*, some $7,000,000 in repairing and rebuilding three thousand tenements in Glasgow, with such good effect that the death-rate fell from fifty-four to twenty-nine per thousand, and crime diminished proportionately.

After *laissez-faire* had been allowed centuries to test its practical effects in educating the masses and had left them in continued ignorance, government began to take the matter in hand. It appropriated £20,000 annually for the education of the poor from about 1830 to 1839, when this pittance was

---

[1] "The State in Relation to Labor." London, 1882, p. 52. The Act re-ferred to is the Factory and Workshop Act of 1878, (41 and 42 Vict. cap. 16), into which previous legislation relating to labor was consolidated.

increased to £30,000. The work has gone on until in the
present decade the final triumph of universal and compulsory
education has been assured. Hon. J. M. Curry, agent of the
Peabody Fund, recently made the following emphatic statement: "I am only stating a truism when I say there is not
a single instance in all educational history where there has
been anything approximating universal education unless that
education has been furnished by government." England has
had no experience which can prove Dr. Curry's assertion an
over-statement.

In our own country it is curious to note how the advocates
of *laissez-faire* abandon position after position. First,
tenements are exempted from what is considered the general
law, because experience has shown that "nothing short of
compulsion will purify our tenement districts." Then it is
discovered that the ordinary laws of supply and demand are
not preserving our forests; consequently, that individual and
general interests do not harmonize. The inadequate action of
competition in regulating and controlling great corporations
gives another excuse for governmental interference. "Cor-
ners" in necessaries of life call for a further abandonment of
the *laissez-faire* dogma, as does also the success attendant on
the establishment of government fisheries. The list might be
extended almost *ad libitum*, and every day adds to it. Thus
has *laissez-faire*, one of the strongholds of past political economy, been definitely abandoned. Justin McCarthy has described, as one of the most curious phenomena of these later
times, "the reaction that has apparently taken place towards
that system of paternal government which Macaulay detested,
and which not long ago the Manchester School seemed in
good hopes of being able to supersede by the virtue of individual action, private enterprise, and voluntary benevolence,"
(Chap. LIV). Legislation is now based to greater extent on
the principle of humanity. Women and children are pro-
tected, not only against the greed of employers, but even
against themselves. Individual freedom is limited both for

individual good and the general welfare.   And as McCarthy has said in another chapter (LXVII.) of his "History of our Own Times": "We are perhaps at the beginning of a movement of legislation which is about to try to the very utmost that right of state interference with individual action which at one time it was the object of most of our legislators to reduce to its very narrowest proportions."

A second practical maxim was deduced from the doctrine of the identity of interests of laborer and labor-giver, which Bastiat, the leader of the optimists, expresses in these words: "Cease, capitalists and workmen, to regard each other with an eye of envy and distrust.   Shut your ears against those absurd declamations which proceed from ignorance and presumption, which, under the pretence of insuring future prosperity, blow the flame of present discord.   Be assured that your interests are one and identical; that they are indissolubly knit together; that they tend together toward the realization of the public good; that the toils of the present generation mingle with the labors of generations which are past; that all who coöperate in the work of production receive their share of the produce; and that the most ingenious and equitable distribution is effected among you by the wise laws of Providence."

Bastiat preaches many little sermons like the one just given, but it is to be feared that their oily properties, if tried, will never reduce the storms of passion to a calm, nor render the riot-act forever an antiquated institution.

If all that Bastiat and his confrères write only held in real life, the solution of the Social Problem would indeed be an easy task.   Business men know, however, that the share of the produce of labor and capital received by labor diminishes by so much the profits of capital, and that, *ceteris paribus,*[1]

---

[1] The two words *ceteris paribus* mean a great deal, but the scope of the present essay does not allow the writer to enter more at length upon the relations between profits and wages.

the larger the proportion of profits received by capital, the
smaller the proportion received by labor. That there is an entire
harmony of interests between the different classes of society, is
at complete variance with the teachings of modern science,
and "is at best a dream of human happiness as it presents
itself to a millionaire."[1] It is possible to reconcile the
different classes of society only by a higher moral development. The element of self-sacrifice must yet play a more
important rôle in business transactions, or peace and good-will
can never reign on earth.

Still another favorite notion of the older economists, and
one which leads to great hardship in real life, is that taxes
are shifted so as to be divided fairly between different employments in which capital is engaged. However convinced
any one might be theoretically of his ability to shift his own
tax upon his neighbor, he would undoubtedly prefer practically to have it laid in the first place upon the neighbor.
"Possession is nine points of the law." This also applies, in
a negative sense, to the possession of an exemption. If landlords are taxed directly, they must first pay the money out of
their pockets; at first, the tenants are free, and the whole
burden of transferring the tax to them rests on the landlords.
But as the tax is imposed in all cases at the same time, there
is a united effort to resist all along the line, and it is almost
certain that the landlords will be obliged to bear at least a
part of it. Besides this, in the case of long leases they bear
the entire burden for years, while the lessees become accus-
tomed to the exemption, and expect it. It is problematical
whether a person ever gets a tax back after he has once paid
it. Taxes ought never to be imposed on the poorer classes,
and when avoidable upon no class of persons, with the idea
that they will eventually free themselves from them.[2] To

---

[1] Gustav Cohn, on "Political Economy in Germany." *Fortnightly Review,*
Sept. 1, 1873.

[2] This does not involve a wholesale condemnation of indirect taxes.

speak of taxation finally righting itself, or of population in the end accommodating itself to the demand for it, and to follow this out practically, would be like the conduct of a general who should choose a busy street in a great capital as a place for his soldiers to practice shooting, and set them to work at once. Some one remonstrates: "But, General, your soldiers will kill people riding and walking in the street." "Very likely," replies he; "at first, some may be killed and some wounded, but in the course of time these matters regulate themselves. People will finally learn to avoid this street. Shoot away, boys!" No, taxes are not paid out of the "hypotheses or abstractions" of the economist.

It is now time to pass over to the more exclusively theoretical side of our argument and inquire into the correctness and sufficiency of the premises of deductive political economy; and the test must be found in the correspondence or non-correspondence of the conclusions logically flowing from the premises with the facts of economic life, for the conclusions must be perfect if the premises are in every respect adequate.

It is natural to consider first the leading premise of the school in question; namely, the supposition that self-interest is the chief force of economic life and that it is, compared with all others, so overwhelmingly preponderating, that the latter are to be considered only incidentally and by way of correction. This is a fair statement, for it gives the *à priori* economists credit for the acknowledgement of modifying causes, or "subordinate causes," as they are termed by Cairnes, who has put the principles of deductive political economy in their most acceptable form.[1] The question, then, is this: Does self-

---

[1] This is more than Lord Sherbrooke (Mr. Lowe) claims. In the article in the *Nineteenth Century,* already referred to (Nov., 1878), he says: "In love, or war, or politics, or religion, or morals, it is impossible to foretell how mankind will act; and therefore on these subjects it is impossible to reason deductively. But once place a man's ear within the ring of pounds, shillings, and pence, and his conduct can be counted on to the greatest nicety. I do not, of course, mean that everybody really acts alike

interest play a rôle in economic life, which corresponds to the
part of a great natural law, like the attraction of gravitation,
everywhere present, everywhere acting with a force to be calculated upon, although subjected to the modifications of subordinate causes? Does it play a rôle in economic life which even
approximates to that of a great natural physical law, which
sets in order and explains a whole world of phenomena?

It is well to begin this inquiry by the examination of
historical phenomena. This will show us that there are entire
great classes of facts, which are quite different from what the
statements of this law by *à priori* economists would lead us to
expect. Self-interest, in the first place, in the sense in which
the word is here used, as equivalent to the desire of wealth, is
often not the force which explains the movements of great
masses. That force is often national honor, devotion to a
principle, an unselfish desire to better one's kind. Let us
take examples from our own history. Twice have we Amer-
icans disappointed in marked manner those who hoped that
our national conduct would be governed by our desire of
wealth, or the almighty dollar. Early in the struggle
between America and England, the British Parliament passed
the act for changing the government of Massachusetts, and
for closing the port of Boston, which took effect June 1, 1774.
This gave the other seaports, and especially Salem, a rare
opportunity to take possession of Boston's trade. Did they
improve it? We will let Webster reply. "Nothing sheds
more honor on our early history," says he, in his speech at
the laying of the corner-stone of the Bunker Hill Monument,
"and nothing better shows how little the feelings and sentiments of the colonies were known or regarded in England,
than the impression which these measures everywhere pro-

---

where money or money's worth is concerned, but that the deviations from
a line of conduct which can be foreseen and predicted are so slight that they
may practically be considered as non-existent. . . . . They may be neglected
without perceptible error."—What becomes of the history of Sparta!

duced in America. It had been anticipated that while the
other colonies would be terrified by the severity of the punishment inflicted on Massachusetts, the other seaports would
be governed by a mere spirit of gain; and that as Boston was
now cut off from all commerce, the unexpected advantage
which this blow on her was calculated to confer on other
towns would be greedily enjoyed. How little they knew of
the depth and the strength and the intenseness of that feeling
of resistance to illegal acts of power which possessed the whole
American people! . . . . The temptation to profit by the
punishment of Boston was strongest to our neighbors of
Salem. Yet Salem was precisely the place where this miser-
able proffer was spurned in a tone of the most lofty self-
respect and the most indignant patriotism."

When our civil war broke out, our enemies declared that it
would be ruinous to our prosperity; if it were continued,
grass would grow in the streets of New York; and the Yan-
kees, ever greedy of wealth, would lay down their arms
rather than suffer such material losses as this would involve.
But the American people again showed their detractors that
there was that which they valued more highly than commercial gain.

But let us take up another great class of economic phenomena, those comprised under the term "wages." Equality
of wages is a perfectly logical deduction from the premises of
à priori economy and moreover one which is constantly recurring in the works of economists. It is true that Cairnes
speaks of "disturbing causes" and ascribes a certain hypo-
thetic character to economic conclusions, but if equality of
wages means anything of value at all, it must denote some
approximation in real life to the absolute equality called for.
What are the facts of the case?

It is idle to ignore the influence of the desire of wealth as
manifested in competition in regulating wages. Our experience of human nature, both of our own and that of others,
and our observation of what happens daily on every side of

us, demonstrate conclusively that the desire of wealth as a
means of obtaining well-being produces a certain tendency
towards equality of wages. But this experience likewise
teaches us that it does not equalize them even in the same
employment in the same country, and does not reduce them
to the lowest possible point in a great number—*possibly* the
majority—of cases. While carpenters are receiving $2.50 in
one place, they receive $3 a day in another locality not a
day's journey distant. Farm laborers in England, in 1873,
received wages which varied from an average of 12*s.* a week,
in the southern counties, to an average of 18*s.* a week, in the
northern—a difference of fifty per cent.;[1] and this difference
was no temporary phenomenon, but appears to have lasted
for years.

The difference in special localities in the north (Yorkshire)
and south (Dorsetshire) of England was still greater, amounting to between two and three hundred per cent. In his
Theory of Political Economy, Jevons, indeed, speaks of forty
different rates of wages in England, and in one place uses
these words: " I altogether question the existence of any such
rate" (*i. e.*, natural rate of wages, such as Ricardo assumed).
"The wages of working men in this kingdom vary, perhaps,
from ten shillings a week up to forty shillings or more; the
minimum in part of the country is not the minimum in
another."[2]

Look hap-hazard where one will, one finds that unequal
wages for similar services are not only paid in places not
remote from one another, but even in the same city or town.
Appleton's Annual Cyclopædia for 1877, for example, gives
the following table of wages paid to engineers and firemen at
the time of the celebrated strike in 1877 :

---

[1] "The Movement of Agricultural Wages in England," Cliffe Leslie in
Fortnightly Review, June 1, 1874. Reprinted in his "Essays in Moral and
Political Philosophy."

[2] Pp. 291–292.

Line of Railroad.	Daily Wages.		Monthly Wages.	
	Engineers.	Firemen.	Engineers.	Firemen.
N. Y. Central, - - - -	$3 15	$1 58	$81 90	$41 08
Erie, - - - - - - -	3 60	2 13	97 12	58 12
Pennsylvania (longer trips—passenger),	3 15	1 80	92 78	51 23
Pennsylvania (shorter trips—freight),	2 34	1 65	83 66	48 03
Illinois Central (passenger), - -	......	......	115 00	57 00
" " (freight), - -	......	......	100 00	54 00
Burlington and Quincy, - - -	......	2 00	81 00	52 00
Lake Shore, - - - - -	2 93	1 47	94 64	47 32

Any reader who still believes that, somehow or other, the theory of equal wages may be true, should consult a document like the Annual Report of the Massachusetts Bureau of Statistics of Labor, for 1883, and ascertain the number of rates of wages paid to unskilled labor in a single state. As the writer glances down one page of the report[1] he finds that the daily wages of ordinary laborers engaged in the manufacture of boots and shoes varied from seventy-five cents to two dollars, seven different rates being mentioned, differing from one another by almost two hundred per cent. And yet a comparison is made between the accuracy of political economy and physics, where a difference which is the thousandth part of one per cent. is noted! Is it not absurd to speak about an equality where such differences exist?

The truth is, other principles than the one of desire of wealth act so powerfully, that it is folly to consider that alone with the expectation of establishing thereby a valuable political economy. In the employment of laborers and servants, the most diverse motives come into play and the desire of wealth is only one of these; others are—generosity, love of mankind, a desire to see those about one happy, pride, sentiment, etc. When a gentleman hires a boy to carry a parcel, he does not haggle with him for five cents; pride restrains him if nothing else. Employers could reduce wages, if they would, in cases not by any means rare. The following two

---

[1] P. 186.

3

cases, which happen to occur to the writer, are given simply as illustrations. A gentleman in New York pays his coachman $50 a month, under the circumstances a high remuneration, and he has no better reason than the purely sentimental one that his deceased father, to whom this servant had been kind, had paid him the same amount. The wealthy proprietor of a widely circulated journal is said to have refused to reduce the wages of his compositors, although the Typographical Union had approved a reduction. He said: "My business is prosperous; why should not my men share in my prosperity?" Friction in economic life is great, and love of home and home surroundings are more potent factors than the desire for wealth.

Professor Cairnes admits an international divergence of profits and wages, sometimes amounting to three and four hundred per cent., which he explains by the various ties which hold one to one's country. But this and similar admissions find no natural place in the old theory of self-interest. It is one of the many self-contradictions in which its adherents inevitably become involved. A philosophical and logical inquiry into the nature of self-interest will make this plain and will clear up one of the fundamental facts of economic life.

It is to be remarked then in the first place that in political economy self-interest may be regarded as a *terminus technicus.* It is in economic life what self-love is in our larger and all-inclusive life. Now self-love is not an evil. It is a good and its exercise is commanded. He who is recognized as first among moral teachers, placed it on a par with love for one's neighbor. The two loves are not contradictory; they find their union in the highest love—love to God. In the same way self-interest in economic life is not incompatible with a conscientious and generous consideration of the material welfare of others. They are both united in the love of humanity. The humanitarian spirit has room for both. Self-interest without consideration for others becomes selfishness, which as essentially different must be distinguished. Selfishness is self-love plus "indifference, disregard for others, enmity and readiness to rob every other individual and the common-wealth;"[1] and, as an evil tree, it cannot bring forth good fruit. It leads to segregation of individuals, separation of classes, distrust, finally mutual hatred, corruption and downfall of the nation. Altruism must and does accompany self-interest and with the progress of individual and national morality, they become ever more closely allied. But altruism without self-interest leads to self-sacrifice, which in the strictest sense of the term self-sacrifice, is immoral. Even when a wider scope is given to the meaning of altruism, it alone cannot possibly serve as an economic guide. It is desirable that as a rule individuals should be dependent upon their own resources most largely for their support and advancement. If I do not support myself, I become dependent upon the labor of others. It is therefore for the interest of society that my self-interest should prompt me to procure those economic goods which are necessary to support life, but always with regard for others. More than this; it is for the general interest that I should advance beyond the state of bare existence, as the progress of the race is inseparable from individual progress. The ideal of economic life then is the union of self-interest and altruism in a broad humanitarian spirit.

Another consideration occurs in this connection. It is impossible to separate the individual from his surroundings in state and society. In the strictest sense of the term and from a purely scientific standpoint, we do not live for our-selves alone but for one another as well as for ourselves. We are inextricably and organically bound up in state and society. What we call self-interest is *as a rule* not interest for one individual. It is a desire for the welfare perhaps of two, three or four united in a family, perhaps of a circle of friends or relatives, perhaps of a town, city, or state. How

---

[1] *Vide* Knies, Politische Oekonomie, 2te Auflage, s. 236.

many men toil for the *ego* alone? Assuredly very few. What
we call egoïsm is usually only relative. We mean the
circle is too narrow. Of course all this does not deny the
existence of such a thing as downright egoïsm or selfishness,
any more than it denies the fact of the existence of robbery,
falsehood, and murder.

All this proves that it is not individual self-interest, certainly not individual selfishness, but *social considerations which
are the first and foremost factor in economic life in modern
times.* It is a social consideration which induces the English
capitalist to prefer " eight or ten per cent. profit with English
society to the quadruple returns of California or Australia." [1]

Consider the bearings of a fact like this. Superior Germans devote themselves to the service of the state in some
way or another and become army officers, civil service offi-
cials or university professors, receive a salary at the height of
their career of from fifteen hundred dollars to thirteen thousand dollars in the rare case of a minister of state, regard their
careers as remarkably successful and look with condescension
upon the millionaire merchant; while in this country the
ablest men have hitherto as a rule devoted themselves to
commercial and industrial undertakings. Now, what is it
which decides the young man of talent in the one country to
seek distinction in the army with the certainty that he will
die a poor man, and the young man of like gifts in the other
to go in quest of the almighty dollar? Is it the desire of
wealth? Assuredly not. The first, the prime motive is the
different social estimate placed upon success in diverse fields
in Germany and America, and this divergence in social estimate is due to historical causes, which no amount of pure
deductive reasoning can ever discover.

Then look at the life of women, who comprise one half of
the human race. Will any one deny that social considerations rather than the desire of wealth shape their lives? Are

[1] Character and Logical Method of Political Economy, p. 49.

not the newspapers continually bewailing the fact that those employments for women which have the shadow of gentility attached to them, are so crowded as to force wages down to a starvation point; while honest and womanly occupations, at all menial in character, but not one whit more arduous, are not sought, though the renumeration offered is excellent?

The economic system, based on the exclusive consideration of self-interest, is full of self-contradictions, as has been shown with sufficient clearness by Professor Knies.[1] Self-interest is called beneficial and exclusive of other motives; yet it is admitted that some men are actuated by higher impulses, which would go to prove that it was neither exclusive nor wholly desirable. Economists maintain that motives of self-interest lead to the most perfect form of society, and, when reproached for this, reply that ethics and religion are correctives. What need of correctives and restraint for that which is good? It reigns in economic life but not in the larger life, that is to say, the same man is controlled in certain spheres of action by one motive and in other spheres by quite a different one; in other words this strange psychology destroys the unity of the mind! As Knies sums it up, "One knows not upon which self-contradiction in this entire doctrine one shall lay most stress in order to demonstrate the uncertainty of the politico-economic laws constructed upon it. Self-interest, it is maintained, is the motive of the economic activity of men—but by no means of all men; it promotes the common welfare—but by no means in all cases; it is, so to say, beneficial in its weakness and injurious in its strength; it controls the economic activity of men—but does not reign outside the economic sphere!"[2]

This Manchester doctrine of self-interest took its origin in French materialistic philosophy of the eighteenth century, is essentially materialistic, and as such is very properly treated by

[1] *Vide* Politische Ockonomie, ss. 229–233.
[2] S. 233.

Lange in his " History of Materialism,"[1] and he rates it below
the philosophic system of Epicurus. When looked at in this
light it does not appear strange that Kingsley applied to it the
epithet, "atheistic."

Not to extend this criticism unduly, only one more point
will be taken up; that of the natural laws of political
economy.

Phrases like natural law, natural right, came largely into
use through the influence of the French philosophy of the
last century. They indicate opinions of an individual or
more generally of a considerable class of persons as to what is
right in itself, in the very nature of things. The difficulty is
a want of harmony as to absolute right between various
nations and between various ages and schools in the same
country. " Right on this side of the Pyrenees, wrong on the
other," is a phrase which points to this divergence. Where
is the infallible guide who is to decide as to natural, social or
economic law? The truth is, the man ventures on very
dangerous ground, who declares a certain form of society or
a given economic institution to be in accordance with the
absolute law of nature. As Bentham calls it, it is usually
"simply dogmatism in disguise." Several years after our
Revolutionary War, the right of the eldest son to receive a
double portion of his father's estate obtained in several of the
states of the American Union, and was spoken of as "being
according to the law of nature and dignity of birthright."[2]

The writer will conclude this division of his subject by a
quotation from a very able paper, by Émile de Laveleye, on
the "Natural Laws and the Object of Political Economy,"[3] and
he is happy to be able to draw to his support in this manner
the able Belgian champion of the new school : " These pretended natural laws are either pure truisms or facts borrowed

---

[1] 3te Auflage, 1866–7, 2ter Bd. ss. 453–483.

[2] G. T. Bispham on Law in America, in *North American Review* for 1876
(vol. 122).

[3] Journal des Économistes, Avril, 1883.

from another order of observations than that with which the economist is occupied. Messieurs Magnin and Maurice Block say to me: But is it not a natural law that man is guided by his own interest? I reply: Yes, in general, but it is not at all necessary in the same sense that the laws of nature are necessary; for frequently man sacrifices his interest to his duty. Besides, that is a postulate furnished to political economy by anthropology. In his speculations, the economist makes use of mathematical laws; he takes notices of the fertility of the soil in treating of rent; of steam, in treating of machines; but all this does not constitute the true object of his science. You may reply further that man must eat to live, and that in order to eat it is necessary to labor and that these are natural economic laws. I reply that they are simply natural facts, which the economist ought not to neglect, . . . but which are borrowed from other sciences. . . . But in the first elements of our researches, see how human institutions and laws modify your pretended natural laws. If there is one law which seems to be imposed upon all organized beings it is that, having the need of nourishment, they must make use of their powers in order to satisfy their wants, and nevertheless in the midst of this social order, which you proclaim natural, this primordial law is violated in virtue of certain institutions which permit the strongest to live without producing anything. . . .

"But is not the great economic law of supply and demand a natural law? Not at all, for Stuart Mill has demonstrated how it is modified by custom. . . . At bottom it is only the truism proved by the experience of all cooks: When fish is scarce, it is dear. In sooth, a beautiful discovery! Nevertheless there is nothing necessary in this. Suppose a religious law which forbids one to eat fish; it might be very scarce and at the same time cheap. . . .[1] Among natural economic laws, M.

---

[1] What Professor de Laveleye says would undoubtedly hold in a country like Brazil, whose whole economic life has for years been essentially modified by religious holidays.

Brants cites, in order to refute me, property;—the most
universal fact of history, cry all the other economists in
chorus.   I study history, and I find on the contrary that
private property in land, such as has been left us by Roman
law, is a recent fact, and that in early times property in the
soil was everywhere collective property. According to this
then, collectivism would be the natural order. . . . Let
us go a little farther. The pivot of all your orthodox political economy and the most natural of your natural laws, is
that man pursues his own interest in everything, and that he
is guided in his actions by the desire of well-being and the
pursuit of wealth. Now there is a political economist of
high merit, and correspondent of the ' Institut,' M. Charles
Périn, who in his work ' De la Richesse dans les Sociétés Chré-
tiennes' (3d edition), claims to demonstrate that it is the principle of renunciation which alone can resolve economic and
social problems. Perhaps he pushes his proposition too far,
but the more I study ancient and modern facts, the more I
find this opinion worthy a serious examination. At all
events, it is certain that the grandest human actions have
been accomplished by humanity under the influence of altru-
istic sentiments. . . . Political economy reduced to the abstract formulae of your natural laws is an emptier scholasti-
cism than that of the Middle Ages. It is on this account
that it has lost credit; not only in Germany and in Italy, but
far more in the land of its birth, England."

All these weaknesses—felt even when not put in words—
and others not enumerated, gradually attracted attention.
Utterances of dissatisfaction with the conclusions of orthodox
political economy, early expressed, became ever more out-
spoken and pronounced with the advance of criticism and the
development of progress, which found no satisfactory explanation in this system. New wine was put into old bottles and
the bottles broke and—perished.

Protest against the harsh doctrines of Ricardo and his followers was early entered by those who were not professional

political economists. Dickens's works are full of such pro-
tests. Nothing, for example, could be more cutting than the
irony with which he describes the principles of the Gradgrind
school in his "Hard Times." Early in the story poor Sissy
Jupe fills them with despair at her stupidity by returning to
the question, "'What is the first principle of political economy?' the absurd answer, 'To do unto others as I would
that they should do unto me.'" Farther on, when poor Gradgrind appeals to his too apt scholar, Bitzer, to admit some
higher motive than self-interest, he is told that "the whole
social system is a question of self-interest. What you must
always appeal to is a person's self-interest. It's your only
hold." Then our author adds: "It was a fundamental
principle of the Gradgrind philosophy that everything was to
be paid for. Nobody was ever, on any account, to give anybody anything, or render anybody any help without purchase.
Gratitude was to be abolished, and the virtues springing from
it were not to be. Every inch of the existence of mankind,
from birth to death, was to be a bargain across a counter.
And if we didn't get to heaven that way, it was not a politico-
economical place, and we had no business there." Frederick
Maurice, the English Christian socialist, Ruskin, and Carlyle
have all condemned in unmeasured terms the "Cobden and
Bright" political economy as detestable. Such expressions,
even, as "bestial idiotism" are used by them in speaking of
free competition as a measure of wages.

Such attacks naturally formed no basis for a reconstruction
of the science, nor was such a basis found in the writings of
political economists like Adam Müller and Sismondi. They
repudiated the Adam Smith school, and gave many good
grounds for their opposition, but they failed to dig deep and
lay broad, solid foundations for the future growth of political
economy. This was also the case with men like Frederick
List and our own Carey. The younger Mill—John Stuart—
occupies a peculiar position. He adhered nominally all his
life to the political economy of his father, James Mill, and

his father's friend, Ricardo. Yet he confesses in his autobiography that the criticism of the St. Simonians with other causes early opened his eyes "to the very limited and temporary value of the old political economy, which assumes private property and inheritance as indefeasible facts, and freedom of production and exchange as the *dernier mot* of social improvement." The truth is, when Mill became dissatisfied with numerous deductions drawn by the leaders of his school, he obtained others, not by investigating and altering the foundation upon which he was building, but by introducing new material, *i. e.*, new motives and considerations, into the superstructure. Mill stood between an old and a new school, having never been able to decide to leave the one or join the other once for all. In political economy he was a "trimmer." This, of course, unfitted him to found a new school himself.

But Mill's scattered expressions of scepticism concerning the value of the deductive political economy and his gradual abandonment of its doctrines, were seed sown, which has sprung up and borne abundant fruit in England; and all this prepared Englishmen to listen when T. E. Cliffe Leslie, filled with German ideas, began about 1870 to attack in unqualified terms the school of *à priori* economists, and these themselves showed a tendency to weaken. Finally the claim of political economy and statistics to form a section of the "British Association for the Advancement of Science" was disputed because their "claims to citizenship in the commonwealth of science" were only "half recognized," and in 1878 at the Dublin meeting of the association, Professor Ingram, president of the section, delivered an address, in which the position of political economy was examined and many of its older methods and principles severely criticized and rejected. This address was published in the proceedings of the association [1] and also in the form of a *brochure* by Longmans, Green & Co., and scattered broadcast the seeds of economic scepticism. Thus it

---

[1] Pp. 641–658 of volume for 1878.

has come to pass that a man like Professor Jevons, who still professed his belief in the possibility of an abstract science of political economy, could in 1879 reject the Ricardian principles in terms as strong as these : " The conclusion to which I am ever more clearly coming is that the only hope of obtaining a true system of economics is to fling aside, once and for ever, the mazy and preposterous assumptions of the Ricardian school. Our English economists have been living in a fool's paradise." The writer has thus sketched the decline and fall of the classical political economy with special reference to England, the home of its birth.

VI.—The New School.

About 1850, three young German professors of political economy, Bruno Hildebrand,[1] Carl Knies,[2] and Wilhelm Roscher,[3] began to attract attention by their writings. The Germans had previously done comparatively little for economic science, having been content for the most part to follow where others led,[4] but men soon perceived that a new creative power had risen. These young professors rejected, not merely a few incidental conclusions of the English school, but its method and the sufficiency of its assumptions, or major premises—that is to say, its very foundation. With their followers, who up to the present have continued to increase in numbers and influence, they took the name Historical School, in order to ally themselves with the great reformers

---

[1] Nationalökonomie der Gegenwart und Zukunft, Frankfurt a/M. Bd. I, 1849.

[2] Politische Oekonomie vom Standpunkte der Geschichtlichen Methode. Braunschweig, 1st ed. 1853. 2d ed. 1881–3.

[3] Grundlagen der Nationalökonomie, 1st ed., Stuttgart, 1859; 16th, 1883. English translation, New York, 1878.

[4] I do not mean that the Germans previous to this time had rendered no services to economic science; such is not the case. But if one examines the work of a man like Rau, up to that time undoubtedly the first German economist, one sees that all the progress made is along the old lines.

in Politics, in Jurisprudence, and in Theology. They studied the present in the light of the past. They adopted experience as a guide, and judged of what was to come by what had been. Their method may also be called experimental. It is in many respects the same which has borne such excellent fruit in physical science. These men did not claim that experiments could be made in the same way as in physics or chemistry. It is not possible to separate and combine the various factors at pleasure; and, although Stanley Jevons has shown conclusively that experiments in social and economic life are not only possible and advisable, but of frequent occurrence,[1] they are always difficult and often cannot be

---

[1] *Vide*, his work, "The State in Relation to Labor," (London, 1882), pp. 23–28, 37, 52, 59; also his essay on "Experimental Legislation and the Drink Traffic," first published in the *Contemporary Review* for February, 1880, then in his collection of essays, entitled "Methods of Social Reform" (London, 1883), pp. 253–276. On p. 256 of this latter work are found these words: "I maintain that in large classes of legislative affairs, there is really nothing to prevent our making direct experiments upon the living social organism. Not only is social experimentation a possible thing, but it is in every part of the kingdom, excepting the palace of St. Stephen's, the commonest thing possible, the universal mode of social progress." Compare with this these sentences from the first-named work (pp. 25–6), "From time to time, too, statesmen have distinctly approved the experimental method. Thus, on 4th March, 1835, Mr. Secretary Goulburn, speaking of the new Factory Act of 1833, said that 'he thought it the most expedient course to make an experiment of the law; so that from actual experience, rather than from contradictory opinions, they might be enabled to ascertain what alterations really were necessary.' In the debate upon the second reading of the Factory and Workshop Bill (11th February, 1878,) Mr. Fielden, whose father was one of the leaders of the party which carried forward the improvement of the Factory Laws, remarked that 'in all its legislation upon the subject, Parliament had been guided by experience, and had gradually extended the operations of the Acts from one trade to another.' In the same debate the Home Secretary expressed his concurrence in the statement that such legislation proceeded on 'a tentative system.' It must be quite apparent, too, that the common practice of passing an Act and then remedying its mistakes, oversights, omitted cases, inconveniences or unforeseen wrongs, in successive Amendment Acts, is really an application of the tentative or experimental method."

made at all as experiments, because the welfare of nations is too seriously involved. But these men claimed that the whole life of the world had necessarily been a series of grand economic experiments, which, having been described with more or less accuracy and completeness, it was possible to examine. The observation of the present life of the world was aided by the use of statistics, which recorded present economic experience. Here they were assisted by the greatest of living statisticians, Dr. Eduard Engel, late head of the most admirable of all statistical bureaus, the Prussian. Hence their method has also been called the Statistical Method.[1] Economic phenomena from various lands and different parts of the same land are gathered, classified, and compared, and thus the name Comparative Method may be assigned to their manner of work. It is essentially the same as the comparative method in politics, the establishment of which Mr. Edward A. Freeman regards as one of the greatest achievements of our times. The method of modern political economy is likewise called Physiological, to call attention to the fact that it does for the social body what physiology does for our animal bodies.[2] Account is taken of time and place; historical surroundings and historical development are examined. Political economy is regarded as only one branch of social science, dealing with social phenomena from one special standpoint, the economic. It is not regarded as something fixed and unalterable, but as a growth and development, changing with society. It is found that the political

---

[1] This name has been sometimes reserved for one wing of the Historical School without sufficient reason. The difference between its various members is simply one of degree.

[2] " Was wir versuchen, ist die einfache Schilderung, zuerst der wirthschaftlichen Natur und Bedürfnisse des Volkes; zweitens der Gesetze und Anstalten, welche zur Befriedigung der letzteren bestimmt sind; endlich des grösseren oder geringeren Erfolges, den sie gehabt haben. Also gleichsam die Anatomie und Physiologie der Volkswirthschaft!" Roscher, National-ökonomie, 14te Auflage, § 26.

economy of to-day is not the political economy of yesterday; while the political economy of Germany is not identical with that of England or America. It is on this account that a knowledge of history is absolutely essential to the political economist. The field of his investigations is the economic life of peoples, and this life is in each case a unity as truly as the life of an individual man is a unity. The life of to-day and yesterday is only a link (Knies). in a great chain; it reaches back into a remote past on the one hand and extends forward into an indefinite future on the other. What is, is closely connected with what has gone before and conditions what is to come. All these parts constitute an organic whole, and it is as impossible to comprehend the economic life of to-day without regard to the past, as it is to understand the body of the full-grown man without a previous study of that of the infant and of the youth. It is the recognition of this intimate and organic relation between history and political economy which renders the title of the new school, the Historical School of Economists, peculiarly fitting. In opposition to the "absolutism of theory" of the political economy of the past, "the historical conception of political economy rests upon this principle: like the conditions of economic life, the theory of political economy, in whatever form found and with whatever argument and conclusions supported, is a product of historical development; it grows out of the conditions of time, place and nationality in vital connection with the entire organism of an historical period; it exists with these conditions and continues to develop with them; it has the source of its arguments in historical life, and must ascribe the character of historical[1] solutions to its conclusions; further all the universal laws of political economy represent only an historical exposition and progressive, advancing manifestation of truth. In every stage of its progress, the theory of political economy is the generalization of truths recognized

---

[1] *I. e.*, relatively, not absolutely true,—valid for certain times and places.

up to a certain point of time, and this theory cannot be declared complete, either as respects its form or substance. When and where absolutism of theory has acquired credit, it must be regarded only as an offspring of the time and as a definite period in the historical development of political economy." [1]

All *à priori* doctrines or assumptions are cast aside by this school; or rather their final acceptance is postponed, until external observation has proved them correct. The first thing is to gather facts. It has, indeed, been claimed that for an entire generation no attempt should be made to discover laws, but this is an extreme position. We must arrange and classify the facts as gathered, at least provisionally, to assist us in our observation. We must observe in order to theorize, and theorize in order to observe. But all generalizations must be continually tested by new facts gathered from new experience.

It is not, then, pretended that grand discoveries of laws have been made. It is, indeed, claimed by an adherent of this school, as one of their particular merits, that they know better than others what they do not know. But it must not, therefore, be supposed that their services have been unimportant. The very determination to accept hypotheses with caution, and to test them continually by comparing them with facts unceasingly gathered, is a weighty one, and promises good things for our future economic development. And in gathering facts, they have been unwearied. Their contributions to our positive knowledge of the economic institutions and customs of the different parts of the world have been wonderful.

An excellent service rendered to science by men of the younger school is a new and undoubtedly more correct interpretation of economic history. The past is not judged by the surroundings of to-day but an effort is made to understand it

---

[1] Knies, Politische Oekonomie, 2d ed., pp. 24–25.

by a sympathetic consideration of its own environments.   In
this manner new light has been thrown upon our studies and
we learn that our fathers have been wiser than we have been
inclined to think, and that it has not been reserved for our
day to discover all that is good and true in the economic life
of nations.   A concrete example of the fruits of this new
method is found in the almost complete reversal of opinion
concerning the policy advocated by those we call Mercantilists.
It is now acknowledged that they were, on the whole, very
shrewd, sensible men, whereas not long since doctrines and
measures were attributed to them, which would lead one to
suppose it necessary to go back only two hundred years to
discover man with a caudal appendage.   The advanced economists have, too, infused a new spirit and purpose into our
science.   They have placed man as man, and not wealth, in
the foreground, and subordinated everything to his true welfare.[1]   They give, moreover, special prominence to the social
factor which they discover in man's nature.   In opposition to
individualism, they emphasize Aristotle's maxim, ὁ ἄνθρωπος
φύσει πολιτικὸν ζῷον, or, as Blackstone has it, "Man was
formed for society."   They recognize, therefore, a kind of
divine right in the associations we call towns, cities, states,
nations, and are inclined to allot to them whatever economic
activity nature seems to have designed for them, as shown
by careful experience.   They are further animated by a fixed
purpose to elevate mankind, and in particular the great masses,
as far as this can be done by human contrivances of an economic nature.   They lay, consequently, stress on the distribution as well as on the production of wealth.

---

[1] This is a return to the conceptions of the Greek philosophers of classical
antiquity. I should say, for example, that if one were to construct a political economy on the basis of the philosophy of Plato, its definition would be
about as follows: Political Economy is the science which prescribes rules
and regulations for such a production, distribution and consumption of
wealth as to render the citizens good and happy.

They watch the growing power of corporations; they study the tendency of wealth to accumulate in a few hands;[1] they observe the development of evil tendencies in certain classes of the population—in short, they follow the progress of the entire national economic life, not with any rash purposes, but with the intention of preparing themselves to sound a note of warning when necessary. If it becomes desirable for a central authority to limit the power of corporations, or to take upon itself the discharge of new functions, as the care of the telegraph, they do not hesitate to counsel it. They make no profession of an ability to solve all economic problems in advance, but they endeavor to train people to an intelligent understanding of economic phenomena, so that they may be able to solve concrete problems as they arise.

One of the most marked features of the political economy of the present is its conception of the organic nature of the economic life of peoples. Reference has already been made to this fundamental fact, and it will now be explained more at length, as the writer conceives it.

The nation[2] in its economic life is an organism, of which individuals, families, groups and even towns, cities, provinces, etc., in their economic life form parts. This is strictly and literally true, as is shown conclusively by comparing the facts of economic life with the ideas embraced in the conception, organism. An organism is composed of interdependent parts, which perform functions essential to the life of the whole. Now a people embraced in one sovereign government together constitute such a whole. The people does not

---

[1] To prevent misunderstandings it is well to state that I speak only of a tendency and say nothing about counteracting forces.

[2] The word is used in the sense assigned to it by Mulford in his admirable work, "The Nation," to denote the people, considered collectively, in a state. It is to be borne in mind that all the United States together, like Switzerland and Germany, constitute one state. A single canton like Geneva, a single state like Prussia, and one of the United States like Pennsylvania are, in an economic sense, less truly states.

4

consist simply of a sum of individuals, nor does the national
economic life—which it is the province of political economy
to investigate—mean a sum of individual economies. This
notion, the fictitious assumption of the classical individual-
istic political economy, holds only of men living in an isolated
barbarous condition, which is a low, mean state of independ-
ence. But the first and foremost factor of modern economic
life is dependence. The phenomena of exchange at once
make this clear. In our advanced society, men do not produce for themselves chiefly, but for others. One man produces shoes and does not consume the hundredth part of what
he produces, while he desires a thousand and one commodities,
which he does not produce. How does he obtain them?
Naturally by exchange. But what must have preceded this
act of exchange? Evidently production on the part of some
one else. Here is the first elementary fact of dependence.
We produce for others, but can obtain from others the satisfaction of our wants only on condition that they produce for
us. The shoe manufacturer may labor never so industriously,
but it avails him not unless others labor. His efforts will
likewise be in vain unless he produces what others want—a
second fact of dependence. He must likewise be able to
induce others to produce such goods as will satisfy his
desires—a third fact of dependence. This is only the beginning. Other men produce the same articles, shoes, and
desire of the remaining members of this organism the same
commodities, *e. g.*, coats, hats, bread, meat, houses, horses,
cows. Here we have briefly indicated four main facts of
dependence. In a society in which production is carried on
for exchange, each producer is dependent upon

1. His own exertions expended in the creation of utilities.

2. The exertions of those who produce commodities which
he desires.

3. Upon the exertions of those who produce the same commodities which he produces; that is to say, upon competition
among sellers.

4. Upon the efforts of others to procure the commodities which he himself desires, that is to say, upon competition among buyers.[1]

As civilization advances, exchanges multiply and dependence increases. The economic life of a civilized people is to-day a most delicate organism, which easily gets out of order, as is seen in constantly recurring crises. Certain parts of this organism then cease to operate satisfactorily, and it becomes apparent how essential to the life of the whole is the performance of the functions of all the parts.

The people of each state constitute an economic organism. The separate laws, national boundaries, both artificial and natural, common systems of taxation, generally common language, to a certain extent common ideas and notions, and a common history comprising common experiences of joy and sorrow,—all act together to divide land from land and to give to each its own peculiar and separate economic existence; in other words, to make of each a separate organism. These separate organisms are connected with each other, and that more closely with the progress of civilization, in particular with improvement in the means of communication. Thus does economic dependence increase not only in intensity, but in extent. If a world-state is ever formed and perpetual peace established, an economic world-organism will doubtless follow. At present it can be said to exist only in embryo, inasmuch as national isolation is still too pronounced.

In opposition to those who would absorb the individual in the state, a fact frequently emphasized by Knies ought to be kept constantly in mind. An economic state-organism is after all different from an organism like a tree or a plant, inasmuch as its separate parts are themselves organisms; of which each has its own ends and is in turn composed of parts, performing their own functions, essential to the existence of the whole. Two simple examples of frequently occurring phe-

---

[1] These four headings are to be found in Knies's "Political Economy."

nomena, will suffice to illustrate the divergence in cases between the interests of the state-organism, and the individual organisms which are its parts. A railroad which benefits the state as a whole may destroy an old family homestead, dear to its owner beyond all money. A lottery injurious to the people as a whole, may be a large source of revenue to an individual.

It may be well in this place to devote a few words to two discoveries of Adolf Wagner, the corypheus of German economists, and the word discoveries is used advisedly; for, though the truths he pointed out are not new in themselves any more than were the Malthusian doctrine of population and the Ricardian theory of rent, they are new in the connection in which they are placed and in the meaning which is put into them. The one discovery is the law of increasing functions of government, and the other is the explanation of the three principles of the economic life of peoples.

Wagner has shown how government has taken upon itself function after function, and how the operations of government trench more and more upon the domain of private industry. This is of the highest importance, as it would lead in time to the absorption of all business by the state, did no counteracting forces begin to act more powerfully than at present.

Whatever our views respecting the first discovery, the second is unquestionable. Wagner has pointed out that there are three essential and distinct principles in all economic life of peoples.

The first is the individual, which was too exclusively dwelt upon by the orthodox political economy. Under this head the powerful and beneficent effects of self-interest as seen in the pursuit of wealth and in its other economic manifestations are sufficiently dwelt upon; and the other facts of private economies (*e. g.*, the principles and phenomena of business life, as it is called), are set forth. The second principle is the social, which acts through the state, and which the socialists,

reasoning on the false assumption that if a little is good, more
must be better, wish to elevate to the reigning and exclusive
principle of economic life.[1] The state corrects, modifies and
rounds out the individual action. Wagner has done meritorious work in his attempts to elucidate the second principle.
He has endeavored to give general norms to determine the
economic functions of the state and he has been successful in
his treatment of certain particular economic functions like the
care and preservation of forests. As he attempts to define the
position of law in political economy and as he always keeps
in mind his social standpoint, he has defined his conception as
the *socialrechtliche Auffasung*—the socio-legal conception, if
it be allowable to coin that word on the model of sociology.
Then follows the caritative principle,—caritative from *caritas*,
love,—the principle of brotherly love, as seen in voluntary
action in behalf of others. Almsgiving is only one form. The
generous deeds of philanthropists are another form this principle takes. It softens the asperities of life and removes hardships from individuals as neither the first nor second could by
any possibility do. Not obliged to operate according to rule
and general law, it takes notice of special cases; it regulates,
modifies and elevates. The need of the time is to develop
into intelligent, harmonious and sufficient activity all three
principles. The preponderance of any one is injurious. The
unintelligent operation of any one is baneful. What is more
admirable than the caritative principle! What more harmful
when it acts without wisdom in indiscriminate almsgiving!

Not the least merit of the younger school consists in this:
they have shown that the attempt to construct a purely theoretical political economy, altogether apart from considerations

---

[1] By the state we mean the political subdivisions of a land as well as the
central authority, comprising the people as a whole. The state is a unity
comprising many subordinate political unities. To all these Wagner gives
the admirable name, compulsory economic communities, Zwangsgemeinwirthschaften. They are coöperative associations resting on a compulsory
basis, in distinction from voluntary coöperative associations.

of policy, is as vain as the search for the philosopher's stone. And the writer cannot, indeed, in this place, resist the temptation to adduce a single example in order to demonstrate in a concrete case that the endeavor to understand the economic life of any people or of any period without respect to legislation is a chimera. The proof and illustration are furnished by the laws of inheritance in England and France. In the latter country, as is well known, the division of landed estates among all the children of a decedent is compulsory by law, whereas in England as a rule the estate goes to the eldest son. What have been the effects on the rural economic life of England and France? In the one country we find land owned in small parcels by numerous peasants, who till their own soil, while in the other we find that the yeomanry, once the pride of England, has disappeared, that the greater part of the soil of England is owned by a small number of wealthy landlords, who let it out to capitalistic farmers, themselves employers of agricultural laborers. These features of England and France, due at least very largely to legal institutions, are among the most marked and those which first attract the attention of the traveler; nor is it doubtful that these differences permeate and change the political and social life of the two lands. Not to attempt to forecast the future, England is to-day decidedly and radically different from what she would be, did not primogeniture obtain in that island, and France is to-day decidedly and radically different from what she would be, were not compulsory and equal division of property among children one of her legal institutions.[1]

In order to obtain a clearer insight into the political economy of the present, the writer will enumerate the more note-

---

[1] Another interesting illustration of the necessity the political economist is under of taking into account legal institutions, is furnished by the laws regulating partnerships. Modern joint-stock companies were, in recent times, illegal in England. What weighty economic consequences have followed the change in the laws which allows their foundation!

worthy articles which have been written for economic journals of late. A definition may mean two things: what is, and what ought to be. An examination of economic journals shows us the subjects which are actually engaging the attention of economists of the present time. It shows "what is" and gives a definition of political economy in that sense. One of the best and most widely circulated economic journals is Conrad's "Jahrbücher für Nationalökonomie und Statistik." The main feature of each issue is one or more essays or monographs, and the subjects of those which have appeared during the year 1882 and 1883 will be enumerated:

1. The Mortality of Infants due to Crime and Poverty and the Importance of this Mortality for the Economic Conditions of Europe.

2. Cause and Effects of a Premium on Paper Money.

3. Trade Unions among the Cigarmakers in Havana.

4. The Cobden Club and German Exports.

5. Labor Time and the Normal Labor Day in the United States.

6. Bimetallism.

7. On Insurance.

8. Income of the Prussian People.

9. The Population of Cities in Earlier Centuries; a study based on the archives of the city of Rostock.

10. On Insurance of Laborers.

11. Treats of some features of Insurance.

12. Reform in Taxation in Germany.

13. Treats of certain Economic Associations in Russia.

14. Forestry and the Economic Life of the People.

15. Population of Brazil in the XVth Century.

16. On German Exports.

17. Trades Unions in the United States.

18. Finances of Prussia.

19. Study of Political Science in America.

20. Bank Note Circulation in Germany.

21. Population of Strassburg from the close of the XVth Century to the Present.

22. Insurance of Laborers.

23. On Ethical Statistics.

The leading French journal of Political Economy is the *Journal des Économistes*, an exponent of the orthodox school. The writer takes up the numbers for 1882, simply because most convenient, and finds that the following are the titles of the leading articles for the first quarter of that year, apart from reviews of publications and reports of various scientific meetings:

1. Finances of Alsace Lorraine.
2. Financial and Economical Situation of the United States.
3. Gold and Silver.
4. The Production and Consumption of Coffee.
5. Agriculture and Manufacturing Industry as affected by Tariff Legislation.
6. Governments and Industry on a Small Scale.
7. Studies upon " Latin " America (New Granada, Venezuela, etc.).
8. Four Labor Congresses.
9. On Method in Economics.
10. Beer, Wine and Spirituous Liquors in England.
11. Economic Poetry of the XVIIIth Century.
12. On the Exchange.
13. The State and the School.
14. Albums of Graphical Statistics of Public Works.

One of the most active economists of England during the last ten or fifteen years was the late Professor Jevons. His two last books were " The State in Relation to Labor," published in 1882, and the collection of essays, published in 1883, bearing the title " Methods of Social Reform," treating of topics like " Industrial Partnerships," " Married Women in Factories," " The Railways and the State." [1]

Perhaps Professor Thorold Rogers, whose *magnum opus* is his " History of Agriculture and Prices," is as promi-

---

[1] A work by him, entitled " Investigations in Currency and Finance," was announced last year.

nent as any living English economist. In an excellent
review of this work, published in *The Nation* of July 20,
1882, Professor Henry C. Adams says: "It is certainly significant, as indicating the present tendency of aggressive work
upon economic subjects, that an author who is able to content himself with a small duodecimo volume, when writing
a 'Political Economy,' should not regard four octavo vol-
umes, averaging seven hundred and forty-five pages each, as
too pretentious when presenting a 'History of Agriculture
and Prices in England,' though it covers three and a quarter
centuries only."

The reader will have observed that the subjects treated of
are mostly such as are embraced under the topics Finance and
Social Problems. In fact, dissatisfaction on the part of social
classes with their condition, and financial difficulties of governments, have ever been the two chief impelling causes of
economic study, and to-day economists are mainly occupied
with them. Scholastic wrangling concerning nomenclature
and verbal quibblings concerning definition have sunk into
comparative insignificance. If regard were had only to "what
is" it would not be very far out of the way to define political
economy as that branch of knowledge which deals with social
and financial problems. But this, although a wide field, is
not sufficiently broad. Political economy, as set forth in
systematic treatises, still deals with generalizations drawn
from economic experience, even when their practical utility
may not be at once apparent; further, with the problem
of premises of economic knowledge; also with nomenclature
and definitions,[1] in order to promote a clear and precise expression of ideas and a better understanding of economic phenomena.

The most recent great work on political economy, which
has been completed, is the "Handbuch der Politischen Oekonomie," edited by Professor Schönberg, of the University of
Tübingen, written by himself in co-operation with twenty-

---

[1] For some interesting remarks on definition, *vide* Sidgwick's article on
"Economic Method," in *Fortnightly Review*, N. S. XXV. (1879), pp. 301-18.

one other economists, each taking that part for which previous study and natural abilities best fitted him. In this work
Professor Von Scheel[1] explains as follows the content and
scope of political economy : " The office of political economy
is to describe the relations of private economies[2] to one
another, their union into larger economic communities, taking
into account their origin and constitution, and to prescribe
norms for the most adequate ordering of these relations,
reference being had to the demands of the degree of civilization attained and to be attained. . . . It has to do with man
as a member of communities. . . . It has to examine the
present constitution, the development and the direction of the
development of that side of the life of a people which is
directed towards the acquisition, the distribution and the consumption of material goods, in so far as this concerns inter-
relations of economic bodies (individual and common, private
and public)."

Characterized more briefly, Political Economy studies
social phenomena from one particular standpoint, viz., that
standpoint which relates to the acquisition, distribution and
consumption of economic goods. Essentially the same conception is conveyed by Knies's definition : " Political Economy
examines the conditions, the processes and the results of the
economic life of men in communities." In the case of both
these definitions, it is tacitly assumed that the economist who
studies and examines economic life, will not neglect to advise
and to prescribe norms for the most satisfactory economic
organism.

The latest important definition of political economy is that of
M. de Laveleye, in his " Éléments d'Économie Politique," published in 1882. It is this:[3] "Political Economy may therefore be defined as the science which determines what laws

---

[1] Bd. I., S. 57.
[2] By economy is meant the entire economic activity of a person or group
of persons ; the efforts put forth to satisfy wants, particularly material wants.
[3] Taken from p. 3 of the English translation, published by G. P. Put-
nam's Sons, New York, 1884.

men ought to adopt in order that they may, with the least possible exertion, procure the greatest abundance of things useful for the satisfaction of their wants, may distribute them justly and consume them rationally." Although, according to M. de Laveleye, political economy seeks to discover "the laws, whether moral, religious, political, civil, or commercial, which are most favorable to the efficiency of labor," it has chiefly to do with legislation, and most economic questions of the day are questions of legislation.   Examples mentioned are "the reform of the laws relating to custom duties, of the land laws, of the laws on currency, of credit, of banking, companies, factory labor, railways, taxation."[1]   "Political economy," adds the same author,[2] "is commonly defined as 'the science which describes the methods of production, distribution and consumption of wealth.'   This definition is altogether inaccurate.   The modes of producing wealth are described in industrial manuals or treatises on agriculture; the mode of its distribution is the subject of statistics; the account of its consumption, the history of the daily life of the various nations."   Though M. de Laveleye's general tendency corresponds to that of the German writers mentioned, he narrows somewhat the scope of the science, in confining it to the search for laws to promote human welfare, and he certainly does not keep within the bounds of his definition in his treatise, some parts of which are merely descriptive and analytic, as the section on the three factors of production, while other portions, like the part treating of rent, deduce conclusions concerning economic phenomena from premises without reference to any question of legislation.   It might be said, perhaps, that rent was connected with private property in land, a legal institution; but this is pushing things too far; and the law of landed property alone is not sufficient to explain rent.

It is seen thus that there is not by any means perfect harmony between the adherents of the younger school; in fact, there are many minor subdivisions and directions of doctrine

---

or tendencies among them. Nevertheless the common features are sufficient to enable one to characterize the school as one great stream of economic thought, quite different from the first great stream represented by the classical political economy.[1]

The method pursued is decidedly inductive in the sense in which that word is used in this paper, and it is well in this place to notice once more a common objection urged against this method. It is said that the facts of economic life are infinite in number and variety, and are quite beyond the grasp of the inductive investigator.

This is plausible, but it overlooks certain marked facts of modern life. If the phenomena of social and industrial life are numerous, so are those numerous in proportion whose business it is to arrange and classify these facts for the student. Let us take up, for example, the subject of national banks in the United States. Certainly a man could never reach any valuable conclusion concerning them by visiting bank after bank and watching people make deposits, or withdraw them, discount bills, calculate interest, &c., &c. The life-time of man is too short. But there are ten thousand bank officers whose life's work it is to watch, arrange and classify facts, which are duly reported four times a year at least to the Comptroller of the Currency, and it is the business of this officer in coöperation with assistants again to

---

[1] No mention has been made of the younger "Mathematical School" of political economists, of whom the chief representatives are Stanley Jevons ("Theory of Political Economy," 2d ed., 1879,) and Léon Walras of Lausanne ("Éléments d'Économie Politique Pure," 1874), because it is difficult to see in their mathematico-economical works anything more than a not very successful attempt to develop further the older abstract political economy. Any advance of the science due to the mathematical character of their method has certainly not as yet become widely known and the writer is much inclined to believe that the works which have advocated the application of mathematics to economics form no essential part of the development of economic literature. Certain unreal conceptions and a few definitions are used as bases for mathematical deductions. When Stanley Jevons treats of practical questions, as in his work, "The State in Relation to Labor," or in his "Methods of Social Reform," his arguments are essentially inductive, and no use is made of the higher mathematics.

sift, arrange, classify and publish these facts, after which they are discussed by the press of this and foreign lands. Even this is not all. Bankers meet in annual convention, disclose their various experiences in formal manner, gather new conclusions from comparison and publish reports to the world. But even this is not all. It is the special function of bankers' magazines to publish from month to month the experience of banks as it occurs, and in this way it is put on permanent record. Thus it is that the economist who wishes to study the phenomena of United States national banks, has at his service a whole army of men who spend their entire time in furnishing him with material in the most convenient shape. Will it then be pretended that it is impossible to study our national banks inductively? This is a single example, but many more might easily be adduced. Insurance is in a similar condition. In Germany an experiment in state insurance of laborers is being made, and it is the business of special functionaries to gather and arrange facts, as they appear. At some future time it will be possible to arrive at a conclusion inductively. English and German factory inspectors are employed, both to enforce factory legislation and to gather and classify facts concerning labor in industrial establishments, which are made accessible to the student. Thousands of men are employed in statistical bureaus, census-offices, clearing houses, chambers of commerce and other similar establishments for the express purposes of gathering, arrangeing and classifying the infinitely varied facts of modern economic life. When the matter is considered in this way, the case of the inductive economist appears by no means hopeless.[1] Doubtless his task is a difficult one, but that is unavoidable. It is on this account that political economy has become a subject too great to be mastered by any one man. Professor Schönberg secured the coöperation of twenty-

---

[1] Cf. Sir George Campbell's address as President of the "Economic Section" of the "British Association for the Advancement of Science" in 1876: published in the Proceedings for 1876.

one men in the preparation of his "Handbuch der Politischen Oekonomie," because "a work which should answer
the demands of science and practical life could be produced
only by the coöperation of many men."[1]

Even Professor Jevons, who was unacquainted with German political economy, and acknowledges he could not read
a German book, was led by an independent course of study
to a similar conclusion. The subject seemed so great to him
that he thought it ought to be divided into several distinct
branches. On this point he says:[2] "The present chaotic
state of economics arises from the confusing together of
several branches of knowledge. Subdivision is the remedy.
We must distinguish the empirical element from the abstract
theory, from the applied theory, and from the more detailed
art of finance and administration. Thus will arise various
sciences, such as commercial statistics, the mathematical theory
of economics, systematic and descriptive economics, economic
sociology and fiscal science. There may even be a kind of
cross subdivision of the sciences: that is to say there will be
division into branches as regards the subject, and division
according to the manner of treating the branch of the subject. The manner may be theoretical, empirical, historical or
practical; the subject may be capital and labor, currency,
banking, taxation, land tenure, etc.,—not to speak of the
more fundamental division of the science as it treats of consumption, production, exchange and distribution of wealth.
In fact, the whole subject is so extensive, intricate and diverse, that it is absurd to suppose it can be treated in any
single book or in any single manner. It is no more one
science than statics, dynamics, the theory of heat, optics,
magneto-electricity, telegraphy, navigation and photographic
chemistry are one science."

The methods and principles of the Historical School have
been continually gaining ground. In Germany they have

---

[1] Vorwort.
[2] Preface to his Theory of Political Economy, p. xvii.

carried the day. The Manchester School may be considered as practically an obsolete affair—*ein überwundener Standpunkt*—in that country. Émile de Laveleye, the Belgian economist, may be named as the most prominent adherent of the school among writers who use the French language, but he has followers of more or less note in France, though the older political economy is stronger there than elsewhere— stronger than in England, its home. Nearly all of the younger and more active Italian economists, as Luzzati,[1] Cossa,[2] Cusumano,[3] and Lampertico,[4] show decided leanings towards the Historical School. These men have learned much from German writers, and Cossa was once one of Roscher's pupils. It is curious to note that they have met with the fate common to all who dare to disturb the repose of the every-day philistine and have been branded by economic orthodoxy as "Germanists, socialists, and corruptors of the Italian youth."[5]

T. E. Cliffe Leslie[6] has led this school in England, and contributed largely to its growth. The most noteworthy English scholars who have openly supported it to a greater or less extent are Stanley Jevons and Prof. Thorold Rogers,

---

[1] A Venetian economist who has written in favor of coöperative societies, people's banks, etc. He was one of the leaders of the Congress of Italian Economists of the younger school which met in Milan in 1875. Its purpose was "to make clear the intentions of those who do not believe the science was born and died with Adam Smith and his commentators."

[2] Author of an excellent little "Guide to the Study of Political Economy," of which an English translation was published by Macmillan & Co., London, 1880.

[3] *V.* Le Scuole Economiche della Germania in Rapporto alla Questione Sociale. Naples, 1875.

[4] Of Vicenza, author of a complete economic course entitled "Economia dei Popoli e degli Stati," Vols. 1–4, Milano, 1874–8.

[5] The accusation of socialism is a common one and has been brought against every economist who has expressed new views from the time of Adam Smith up to the present. Whenever a man, into the darkness of whose mind an original idea never penetrated, is confronted with economic doctrines at all strange or new, he is ready to condemn them at once with the cheap reproach of "socialism."

[6] *V.* Essays in Moral and Political Philosophy, London, 1879.

whose monumental work on "Agriculture and Prices," written
in the spirit of that school, has excited world-wide admiration. The younger men in America are clearly abandoning
the dry bones of orthodox English political economy for the
live methods of the German school. We may mention the
name of Francis A. Walker, the distinguished son of Amasa
Walker, as an American whose economic works are fresh,
vigorous, and independent. Essentially inductive and historical in method, they have attracted wide attention and
favorable notice on both sides of the Atlantic.

This entire change in the spirit of political economy is an
event which gives occasion for rejoicing. In the first place,
the historical method of pursuing political economy can lead
to no *doctrinaire* extremes. Experience is the basis; and
should an adherent of this school even believe in socialism as
the ultimate form of society, he would advocate a slow
approach to what he deemed the best organization of mankind. If experience showed him that the realization of his
ideas was leading to harm, he would call for a halt. For he
desires that advance should be made step by step, and opportunity given for careful observation of the effects of a given
course of action. Again: this younger political economy no
longer permits the science to be used as a tool in the hands of
the greedy and the avaricious for keeping down and oppress-
ing the laboring classes. It does not acknowledge *laissez-
faire* as an excuse for doing nothing while people starve, nor
allow the all-sufficiency of competition as a plea for grinding
the poor. It denotes a return to the grand principle of common sense and Christian precept. Love, generosity, nobility
of character, self-sacrifice, and all that is best and truest in
our nature have their place in economic life. For economists
of the Historical School, *the political economy of the present,*
recognize with Thomas Hughes that " we have all to learn
somehow or other that the first duty of man in trade, as in
other departments of human employment, is to follow the
Golden Rule—' Do unto others as ye would that others
should do unto you.'"